# A DAY IN AN ECOSYSTEM

# 24 HOURS IN A POND

## VIRGINIA SCHOMP

Cavendish Square

New York

Published in 2014 by Cavendish Square Publishing, LLC
303 Park Avenue South, Suite 1247, New York, NY 10010

Website: cavendishsq.com

This publication represents the opinions and views of the author based on his or her personal
experience, knowledge, and research. The information in this book serves as a general guide only. The
author and publisher have used their best efforts in preparing this book and disclaim liability rising
directly or indirectly from the use and application of this book.

CPSIA Compliance Information: Batch #WS13CSQ

All websites were available and accurate when this book was sent to press.

Library of Congress Cataloging-in-Publication Data
Schomp, Virginia.
24 hours in a pond / Virginia Schomp.
p. cm. — (a day in an ecosystem)
Includes bibliographical references and index. Summary: "Take a look at what takes place within a 24-
hour period in a pond. Learn firsthand about the features, plant life, and animals of the habitat"—
Provided by publisher.
ISBN 978-1-60870-894-9 (hardcover) ISBN 978-1-62712-067-8 (paperback)
ISBN 978-1-60870-901-4 (ebook)
1. Ponds—Juvenile literature. I. Title. II. Title: Twenty four hours in a pond.
QH98.S36 2013
577.63—dc23
2011041778

Editor: Peter Mavrikis
Art Director: Anahid Hamparian
Series Designer: Kay Petronio
Photo research by Alison Morretta

Printed in the United States of America

# CONTENTS

# FIRST THINGS FIRST

Ponds are a great place to explore, but remember—be smart and stay safe. Always take an adult with you. Never go into the water alone. And leave the plants and animals as you find them. After all, you wouldn't want a dragonfly to come and mess up *your* place!

# DAWN

**THE SUN** is rising on a bright day in early summer. You walk down a shaded path and come to a **pond** surrounded by bright green grasses, flowering shrubs, and tall trees. The water is smooth as glass. It seems peaceful and calm. But look closely and you will discover a busy world teeming with life.

Ponds are small, shallow bodies of water. They do not flow like rivers. They are not as big as lakes. Their waters can be home to many different kinds of plants and animals that could not survive in a rushing river or a deep, cold lake.

How do these small worlds get their start? Ponds can form in many different ways. The water from melting ice and snow may collect in a hollow in the ground. A river may overflow during a flood. A lake can even turn into a pond as it slowly fills up with dirt.

◀ Early-morning clouds reflect off the calm waters of a pond.

A busy beaver adds a stick to its wet, muddy dam.

Ponds also may form when a dam blocks a river or stream. The water backs up behind the dam and spills over the surrounding land. Some dams are created naturally, from falling rocks or a mudslide. More often, dams get a helping hand. People may block a stream to make a pond in a park or backyard. A beaver may build a dam from logs, branches, and rocks. The shallow water below the beaver dam becomes a home for the builder and many other pond creatures.

Ponds are found nearly all over the world. Today you are exploring a beaver pond in New York. Some of the plants and animals that live here will be easy to find. Some are so tiny that you cannot even see them without a microscope. No matter their size, they are all a big part of the small, busy world of the pond.

## LAKE OR POND?

How big can a pond be before we call it a lake? There is no exact answer. One way to tell the difference is to look at the plants. Sunlight reaches the bottom of ponds, so plants can take root there. Plants do not grow in lakes, except in the shallow waters near the shore. Another difference is temperature. A lake can be warm at the top and cold at the bottom. The water temperature is about the same everywhere in a pond.

# MORNING

**ARE YOU WEARING** your wading boots? It is time to explore the different parts of the pond. And in this watery world, that will mean getting wet.

Even a small pond has several **zones**. A zone is a part of the pond with its own special conditions. Each zone is home to its own types of plants. Some animals live in only one zone, but most roam all over the pond.

Your tour starts in the **swamp zone**. This is the part of the pond that is closest to the shore. The water is shallow. Tall grasses and hollow-stemmed reeds and cattails reach toward the sunlight.

Wade out a little deeper. Now you are in the **floating leaf zone**. It is easy to see how this part of the pond got its name. The leaves of most of the plants float on the surface of the water. Some of the floating leaves

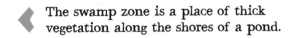

The swamp zone is a place of thick vegetation along the shores of a pond.

Lily pads float on the surface of the pond.

are as big and round as dinner plates. These "lily pads" are the leaves of water-lily plants. Fat roots anchor the plants in the mud at the bottom of the pond. A stretchy stalk connects the roots to the leaves and sweet-smelling flowers.

You will have to slosh out even farther to explore the **submerged plant zone**. Here the plants grow almost completely underwater. Waterweeds and water violets send their roots down into the mud. Their feathery stems and leaves sway gently in the water. Only their flowers may peek out above the surface.

Near the center of the pond is the **free-floating plant zone**. The plants in this group are not rooted in the mud. Instead, they are free to float on the surface. Some free-floating plants have no roots at all. Others have long, thin roots that dangle in the water.

Free-floating plants sometimes spread over large areas of the pond. Tiny duckweeds may cover the water from shore to shore. Insects and spiders scurry around on the floating carpet.

Free-floating duckweeds grow in dense clumps on still, shallow water.

Why are cattail stems hollow? What makes lily pads float? How can waterweeds grow underwater without turning mushy? The answer to all these questions is **adaptation**. The plants have adapted, or changed in ways that help them survive in their part of the pond.

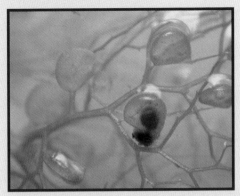

An insect trapped inside a bladderwort plant

## BEWARE THE PLANT!

Most pond plants get their food from the water. The bladderwort is different. It eats insects! The leaves of this free-floating plant have tiny pouches called bladders. The bladder opening is surrounded by hairs. When an insect touches the hairs, a trapdoor opens. The insect is sucked inside. Then the door snaps shut, trapping the plant's meal.

Swamp-zone plants have long, strong roots to hold them up in the shallow water. But roots need **oxygen** to grow—and there is not much oxygen in the soggy ground. Hollow stems solve the problem. The reeds and cattails use their stems like a pipe to send oxygen down to their roots.

Water lilies grow in deeper water, so they need different adaptations. The lily pads are waxy on top. Water runs off, so the leaves will not get heavy and sink. Hollow spaces in the leaves and stems hold air and help the plants float.

Submerged plants have the most adaptations to life in the water. Can you see the feathery stems of the waterweed? If you put this plant on land, it would collapse. It does not need strong stems in the pond, because the water supports it.

Plants that grow underwater do not need strong roots either. Land plants use their roots to take in food and water from the soil. Submerged plants are surrounded by water filled with **nutrients**. Every part of the plant—leaves, stems, and roots—can drink in the feast.

You must take off your boots to discover another plant adaptation. Now wriggle your toes gently in a clump of waterweeds. Yuck! Can you feel the slimy coating on the stems and leaves? The slime keeps out some of the water, so the plant does not get too soggy.

The tall grasses have scratched your arms. Duckweeds are sticking to your legs. It would be hard to miss these pond plants. But the pond is also filled with millions of simple plantlike organisms called **algae**. Some algae are the size of a freckle. Many are even smaller. You can only see these tiny organisms when they clump together in large greenish patches.

Algae live all over the pond. They attach themselves to stones, twigs, and plants. They lie on the muddy bottom and float on the surface. On hot, sunny days, they can multiply very quickly. A thick mass called an "algae bloom" covers the surface like a slimy green blanket.

Algae are not the only super-small life forms in the pond. There are also many types of **fungi** and **bacteria**. Some fungi and bacteria cause sickness. Others help keep the pond clean by feeding on the remains of dead plants and animals.

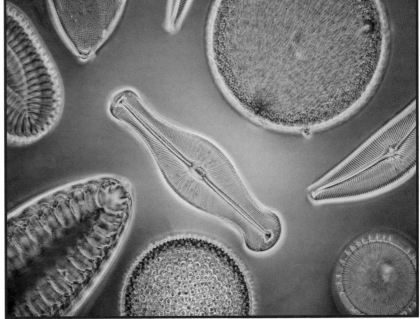

Tiny pond algae can look beautiful under the microscope.

## PHOTO-WHAT?

*Photosynthesis* is a big word made up of two smaller parts. *Photo* means "light." *Synthesis* means "combine." In photosynthesis, plants use *light* energy to *combine* water and a gas called **carbon dioxide**. That produces a kind of sugar that the plants use as food.

Tiny algae. Small duckweeds and tall cattails. Insects and frogs and beavers. All the living things of the pond form a **community**. All the members of the community are linked by a **food chain**. When we study the food chain, we can see how energy passes from one living thing to another.

It all starts with the sun. Plants collect energy from sunlight. Through a process called **photosynthesis**, they use that energy to make food. Because they make their own food, they are known as "producers."

Animals are the "consumers" of the food chain. They cannot make their own food, so they must consume other living things. Plant-eating animals eat plants. Meat-eating animals eat the plant-eaters. Bigger meat-eaters eat the smaller ones.

Fungi and bacteria are **decomposers**. They break down dead plants and animals into smaller parts. The food energy in the plants and animals returns to the water, where it helps living plants grow.

Most pond animals eat more than one kind of food. That means each animal can be part of more than one food chain. All the food chains together make up a **food web**. The food web is like a spiderweb with many overlapping strands. All the living things in this web of life and death depend on one another for survival.

## THE BREATH OF LIFE

During photosynthesis, plants produce oxygen. Nearly all living things need oxygen to survive. On a sunny day, you may see streams of bubbles rising to the surface of the pond. These are a sign that the plants are pumping out lots of oxygen.

# AFTERNOON

**THEY FLY.** They swim. They dive under the water. They scurry around on the surface. And . . . *ouch!* Some of them bite!

Thousands of different types of insects and other small creatures live in ponds. Each **species** has its own ways of coping with life in the water. Some adaptations help animals move around. Others help them get oxygen. Still others make it easier to find food—or to keep from becoming food for some other pond dweller.

The sun is right overhead. The pond is warming up. Colorful butterflies and dragonflies bask in the sun. Tiny midges and mosquitoes rest in the shade of the willow trees.

Out on the pond surface, a water strider is on the prowl. The little insect skates around until it feels a small vibration. A spider has fallen into

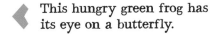

This hungry green frog has its eye on a butterfly.

Oily hairs help the water strider glide around on the surface film.

the water! With a quick hop, the water strider captures its **prey**. It grabs hold with its front legs, inserts its sharp beak, and sucks the spider dry.

How can the water strider skate on the water? It takes advantage of something called **surface tension**. Surface tension happens when a body of water meets the air. The water acts like it has a thin elastic skin stretched over the top. Small, light animals can move around on the surface film without getting wet.

The water strider is well adapted for life on the surface film. This small **predator** can move as fast as 60 inches (150 centimeters) a second. It rows over the water with its two long middle legs. Its two back legs handle the steering. Its lower body is covered with oily hairs that trap air bubbles and help it stay afloat.

The water strider glides past a water measurer. This sticklike insect has no need for speed, because most of its food is already dead. It tiptoes slowly over the surface on its long, thin legs. It spots a dead fly floating on the water. What a yummy treat! The water measurer stabs the fly with its sharp beak and slurps up the body juices.

A group of whirligig beetles are stirring up the surface. The shiny black beetles whirl around one another like spinning tops. Whirligigs live half in and half out of the water. Their waterproof backs rise above the surface. Their bottoms sink below. Their legs are short and flat, for paddling around in the water.

Whirligig beetles are named for the way they whirl around on the water.

## POND SALAD

Some insects eat meat, and others eat plants. A few chow down on both. The water boatman swims with its oarlike back legs. Its front legs end in little "spoons." These are the perfect tools for scooping up food from the pond bottom. The soggy salad includes algae, bacteria, and other tiny plants and animals.

As they swim, whirligig beetles look for insects to eat. They also watch out for hungry predators. Birds can attack from the air. Fish can strike from below. No problem! This bug's eyes are divided into upper and lower parts. That lets a whirligig look up and down at the same time. If it spots an enemy, it dives down and hides among the plants. The beetle carries an air bubble under its belly. It breathes the air in the bubble the same way a scuba diver uses an air tank.

Whirligig beetles have one more defense against predators. They can coat their skin with a bad-tasting goo. A fish that gets a mouthful of whirligigs may spit them out. The next time the fish goes hunting, it will look for a more appetizing meal.

A water scorpion pokes its breathing tube up through the surface film.

Whirligig beetles carry their own air. How do other small pond creatures breathe underwater? Many insects have **gills**, like a fish. The gills absorb oxygen from the water. Others have long breathing tubes that stick out above the surface.

A few baby flies and beetles get their air from submerged plants. They insert tubes into air-filled spaces in the stems and roots.

The fishing spider rests on a floating leaf. It waits for a tasty insect or fish to wander by. Sometimes the spider has to chase its prey under the water. Then it breathes air trapped in the short, velvety hairs covering its body.

Sludge worms are decomposers. They bury their heads in the mud to feed on bits of decaying plants. While the worms feed, they wiggle their tails. The tails act like a gill, extracting oxygen from the water.

A bright purple insect hovers over the warm water. Its long wings sparkle in the sunlight. Then *whoosh!* The dragonfly darts off to catch a juicy mosquito.

Adult dragonflies spend most of their time in the air. But like all pond insects, these flying jewels start their lives in the water. The series of

A water spider with an air bubble

# LIFE IN A BUBBLE

The water spider lives in ponds in Europe. It is the only spider that spends its whole life underwater. The small brown spider spins a silk web between submerged plants. It brings down air bubbles from the surface and puts them inside its "air bell." It keeps adding silk and air until the shelter is big enough to live inside.

changes that takes them from egg to adult is called **metamorphosis**.

Female dragonflies lay their eggs in the water or on leaves. Soon the eggs hatch. Out come the **nymphs**. These small, fat babies are the terror of the pond. They eat other insects, tadpoles, and small fish. A nymph catches its prey with its long lower lip. The lip shoots out like an arm. Deadly hooks on the lip snag the victim and drag it to the nymph's mouth.

Dragonflies may spend several months or years as nymphs. Every few months, the nymph molts. It sheds its hard outer skin and steps out in a

A female dragonfly lays her eggs on a twig at the water's surface.

new, larger one. Each time it molts, it looks more like an adult dragonfly.

Finally, it is time to leave the water. The nymph climbs out onto a leaf or twig. Its skin splits for the last time. The adult dragonfly crawls out. Its four wings slowly unfold, and it takes to the air. It will only live a few weeks—just long enough to mate and start the next generation of dragonflies.

## THE MAGIC OF METAMORPHOSIS

Most young insects that live on the land look like tiny adults. In the pond, baby insects may look nothing like their parents. Why the difference? The pond babies live completely underwater. They need special ways to get food and oxygen. When they grow up, they will spend time out of the water, so they will need different adaptations.

# EVENING

**THE SUN** is getting low in the sky. As the day cools down, insects swarm over the pond. *Splash!* Look quickly and you will see a silvery flash. A sunfish is leaping from the water. In one gulp, the fish swallows a dragonfly. Then it disappears beneath the surface.

Insects are an important part of the pond food chain. They are food for birds, frogs, and nearly every kind of fish. These big predators in turn are eaten by larger meat-eaters, from snakes to snapping turtles to raccoons.

With their patches of blue, green, yellow, orange, and red, sunfish are some of the most colorful fish in the pond. And now is a great time to see them. Sunfish rest during the hottest part of the day. In the cool of the evening, they come out to feed.

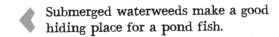 Submerged waterweeds make a good hiding place for a pond fish.

Sparkling colors and patterns help the bluegill blend in with its watery surroundings.

Keep your eye on the surface. A bluegill sunfish is searching for food. This brightly colored fish eats both meat and plants. First it nibbles on some snail eggs stuck to the underside of a lily pad. Then it swallows a grasshopper that took a wrong turn and landed in the water. The fish rounds out its meal with a bite of slimy algae.

You are not the only one watching the bluegill. A largemouth bass is hiding behind some weeds in the shallow water. The bass is a type of sunfish, too. But this top predator is twice as big and heavy as the bluegill.

The bass waits for the smaller fish to swim near. Then it dashes out with its huge mouth wide open. The startled bluegill takes off. It zigs and zags through the water. After a minute, the bass gets tired and ducks back into its hiding place.

How can the bluegill swim so fast? Why does the largemouth bass have such a big mouth? Each fish has adaptations that make it a pro at pond living.

The bluegill spends a lot of time searching for food and fleeing from predators. Its flat, slender body helps it move quickly and easily through the

The largemouth bass has powerful jaws for catching its prey.

## FISHY FATHERS

When the water warms up in summer, bluegills start a family. The male fish build a nest in shallow water. The females lay the eggs. Then the fathers-to-be stand guard. They attack anything that comes near the nest. They keep up their watch until the eggs hatch and the babies swim off to live on their own.

## MOUTH BREATHERS

Just like you, fish breathe oxygen. But they do their breathing underwater. A fish sucks in a mouthful of water. It forces the water over its gills. Tiny blood vessels in the gills absorb the oxygen and release carbon dioxide. The "used" water passes out through gill slits on the side of the fish's head.

water. Special notched fins let the fish speed up, turn, and brake in the blink of an eye.

The largemouth bass is bigger and more muscular. This fish is built for short bursts of speed. It hides behind cover and strikes fast. If its prey gets away, it settles back to wait for a less troublesome meal.

That huge mouth lets the bass capture other big fish and frogs. It can also "inhale" smaller prey. When the bass snaps its mouth open, a gush of water rushes in. So do all the critters floating in the water. Like many fish, the bass has bony fringes attached to its gills. These "gill rakers" comb the water, trapping tiny bits of food. The bass swallows its snack, and the water passes out through its gill slits.

As you explore the pond, you will see fish with all sorts of other adaptations. Fish that feed near the surface often have upturned mouths. Bottom-feeders have mouths on the underside

A pike uses its sharp, curved teeth to gobble up a smaller fish.

of the head. These fish may have whiskers, too. It is hard to see food on the muddy bottom. Whiskers help the fish feel for a meal.

A fish's teeth can give you other clues to its eating habits. Pike have sharp teeth that point backward for holding on to large prey. The pumpkinseed's teeth are strong and blunt. That lets this small sunfish crunch up its favorite food, snails. The grass carp has grooved teeth in the back of its throat. This fish eats only plants. Plants are hard to digest, so the grassie uses its "throat teeth" to shred its meals.

Most fish have a swim bladder. This body part is like an air-filled balloon

## SNAIL TRAILS

Snails have a foot, but it is not like yours. The snail's foot is a muscular organ on its bottom. The snail wriggles its foot to make waves that push it forward. It produces a trail of slime to make moving easier. The slime is so sticky that a pond snail can glide upside down on the surface film.

that allows the fish to float. Fish add air to their swim bladder to rise and take out air to sink.

A catfish called the brown bullhead has another use for its swim bladder. If the pond dries out, the bullhead buries itself in the mud. While it rests quietly, its swim bladder absorbs oxygen from the air. This hardy fish can survive for weeks while it waits for the rains to come and fill up the pond again.

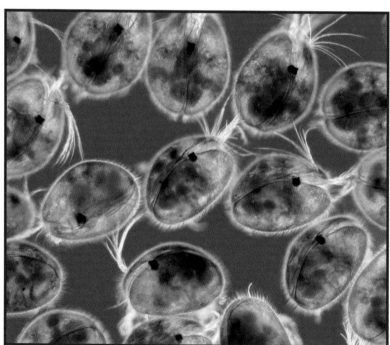

Under the microscope, seed shrimp look like feathery beans.

A pond snail creeps over a stone. It is scraping up bits of algae with its rough tongue. Uh-oh! Here comes a hungry sunfish. In a blink, the snail pulls its soft body into its cone-shaped shell.

Shrimp have shells, too. Most shrimp live in the ocean, but a few species are adapted to the freshwater in ponds. Side-swimmer shrimp swim by beating the legs on their bellies. Seed shrimp row with their antennas. These little shrimp grow to only about one-eighth of an inch (3 millimeters) long.

Many pond creatures are even smaller than the seed shrimp. Water fleas get their name from the way they "hop" through the water like fleas. Copepods (KOH-puh-pods) are related to shrimp, but these tiny swimmers have no shell. Rotifers have a "wheel" attached to their mouth, but you will need a microscope to see it. The miniature wheel is really a circle of hairs used for swimming and feeding.

All these creatures are part of the pond **plankton**. Plankton includes masses of very small plants and animals that float in the water. Many insects feed on plankton. Many fish filter the floating feast out of the water with their gill rakers.

How can a plankton animal keep from getting eaten? One way is to stay on the move. During the day, plankton animals sink down to the deeper waters, where they are harder to see. At night, they rise to the surface to feed on the other tiny plants and animals in the plankton.

# NIGHT

**LARGE** animals may divide their time between the pond and dry land. Birds stop by for a drink or a meal. Some snakes and turtles hunt in the water and sun themselves on shore. Frogs and toads can hop around on land, but they must stay near the water to keep their skin moist.

*Chi-chi-chi-chi.* You hear a rattling call. Look up and you will see a belted kingfisher perched on a branch above the water. Night is coming. There is time for just one more snack before the bird goes to bed. Suddenly the kingfisher takes off. Its blue wings flash as it dives headfirst into the pond. It comes up holding a small sunfish in its beak.

The kingfisher is one of many birds that may depend on the pond for food. Long-necked swans and noisy ducks and geese nibble on the plants. Warblers peck at insects. Long-legged herons wade out to catch

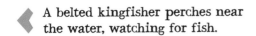
A belted kingfisher perches near the water, watching for fish.

The great blue heron wades out into the pond to catch its meals.

fish. A red-shouldered hawk watches for frogs, snakes, and mice. This bird is a skilled hunter. Keen eyesight, a strong hooked beak, and razor-sharp talons help it snag its prey.

Ponds also make a good nesting place. Watch quietly and you may spy the entrance to the kingfisher's nest. The little bird was not hunting for itself. It was getting food for its hungry chicks. It flies to a hole in the side of a hill near the water. Five baby birds wait in a chamber at the end of the tunnel. The chicks were born blind and featherless. Their parents will watch over them for about four weeks. After that, the babies will learn how to take care of themselves.

As darkness settles in, noises fill the air. *Chirp! Peep! Gr-rum! Twa-a-a-ng!* What is this strange chorus? The frogs are waking up. Some frogs are active in the daytime, but most are **nocturnal**. Nocturnal animals rest during the day and come out at night.

You will need your flashlight—and a quick eye—to catch sight of a bullfrog. When you walk near, that deep *gr-rum* turns into a *splash* as the frog leaps into the water. Long hind legs make this frog a champion jumper. Some bullfrogs can leap ten times their body length.

If you *could* get close to the bullfrog, you would find that its skin is moist. Frogs have lungs to breathe air, but they also breathe through their skin. The frog sits in the shallow water. It absorbs oxygen from the water that seeps through its skin. The skin has to stay moist to take in oxygen. If it dries out, the frog will die.

A big leap can help the bullfrog catch its prey or escape from a hungry predator.

A young kingfisher with a fish.

## FISHING LESSONS

When baby kingfishers leave the nest, their parents teach them how to find food. The parent bird catches a small fish and whacks it on a branch. It drops the stunned fish into the water. After a while, the chicks get the idea. One by one, they learn how to dive into the pond and catch their supper.

## DOUBLE LIVES

Frogs, toads, and salamanders are **amphibians**. These animals begin their lives in the water. When they are grown up, they can live on the land. Even when they are adults, amphibians must stay near water so their skin does not dry out.

Frogs also need water to make more frogs. In the spring and early summer, male frogs sing to attract a mate. The female frogs lay their eggs in the pond. The eggs hatch into tadpoles. The tadpoles look more like little fish than frogs. They even breathe through gills like a fish.

As the tadpoles get older, they grow legs. They lose their gills and develop lungs. Some frogs need only a few months to complete their metamorphosis. The bullfrog can take three years to grow from tadpole to adult.

At last, the frog is ready to take its first hops on land. It hides among the plants at the pond's edge. *Flick!* It snags a beetle with its long, sticky tongue. *Gulp!* A mouse disappears into the bullfrog's mouth.

A painted turtle crawls toward the pond. The small, colorful turtle has just finished laying her eggs. She dug a nest in a sandy spot near the shore. She laid six white eggs and covered them with dirt. Later this summer, the eggs will hatch. The baby turtles will dig their way out of the nest and scurry to the water.

Painted turtles have webbed feet for paddling around the pond. They dine on plants, insects, worms, and snails. The snapping turtle has more on the menu. This large turtle will eat fish, frogs, snakes, and anything else it can catch with its strong, sharp beak.

Large or small, all turtles are cold-blooded. That means their body temperature changes with the temperature around them. A few times a day, they must leave the water to warm up. The turtle climbs onto a rock or log and soaks up the sun.

Snakes are cold-blooded, too. When the sun is out, the northern water snake slithers through the tall water grasses. It searches for fish, frogs, salamanders, and other small animals. The snake's dull coloring blends in with its surroundings. This **camouflage** helps it hide from both predators and prey.

After a cool swim, a painted turtle warms up by basking in the sun.

You point your flashlight at the pond's edge. Dozens of bright yellow eyes stare back. A mother raccoon is teaching her babies

## THE POND IN WINTER

How do cold-blooded pond animals get through the winter? Snakes crawl into a hole. Turtles and frogs bury themselves in the mud. They all go into a deep sleep called hibernation. Some insects hibernate, too. Other insects and fish stay active, but they move more slowly in the cold water beneath the ice.

how to find their supper. Last night, she introduced them to berries, worms, and grasshoppers. Now she pounces into the shallow water and comes up with a wriggling fish.

The raccoon is not the only **mammal** to visit the pond at night. You might see white-tailed deer nibbling on the leaves and grasses. Mouselike shrews hunt for worms, insects, and snails. The shrew's hair repels water, so it can go for a swim and come out dry.

A white-tailed deer grazes on plants at the pond's edge.

Muskrats eat plants, snails, frogs, and turtles. These furry animals look like small beavers, but their closest cousins are rats and mice. A family of muskrats may use cattails to build a small dome-shaped lodge in the water.

The most famous builders in the pond are the beavers. This pond was created when a pair of beavers dammed a stream running through the woods. The stream overflowed into a low-lying meadow. Then the beavers built their lodge in the still, shallow water.

The beaver lodge looks like a mound of sticks in the middle of the pond. Inside is a dry living chamber. The beavers swim in and out through tunnels under the water. Their island home is a safe, comfortable place to eat, sleep, and raise a family.

Beavers work on their lodge at night. Do you see that big, brown animal towing a branch through the water? With its waterproof fur, webbed feet, and broad tail, the beaver is an excellent swimmer. It drags the branch up the side of the lodge. It dives down into the water. It comes up with a load of dripping mud to cement the branch in place.

While the father beaver repairs the lodge, the mother is taking care of the babies. She cuts down a small maple tree with her long, sharp teeth. She drags the tree to the edge of the pond, where four young beavers are waiting. The babies quickly gobble up the leaves and bark. All summer

The thick walls of a lodge keep beavers safe from wolves, bears, and other hunters.

long, the parents will work to store branches and twigs for their growing family to eat during the winter.

The beavers swim into their lodge to sleep. The raccoons snuggle down in their den. Night is coming to an end. Soon the birds will sing up the sun. Fish will dart through the water. Insects will swim and dive, fly through the air and crawl on the pond's muddy bottom.

All these creatures are an important part of the pond **ecosystem**. And that small ecosystem is important to us all. A sunlit pond can have more types of plants than even the richest grasslands. It can be home to an amazing variety of animal life.

Ponds are valuable in other ways, too. They help prevent floods by holding rainwater. Soil that would be washed away in a flood settles to the bottom of the pond. Decomposers feed on the animal waste and other pollution. If the water is not too dirty, the pond will clean it up in time.

But pollution can also destroy ponds. Chemicals can poison the water. Then the plants and animals may not grow properly, or they may die. Fertilizers and other wastes can overload the

The chemicals in these old barrels can harm raccoons and other animals that depend on the pond for water and food.

## FROG SCIENTISTS

Frogs are a good **warning sign.** Their skin takes in oxygen from the air and water. Dirty air or water can kill the frogs or keep tadpoles from growing into healthy adults. When that happens, scientists know there is something wrong with the ecosystem. They study the frogs to find the problem and figure out how to fix it.

water with nutrients. Algae multiply until they cover the pond, blocking the sunlight and killing plants. Bacteria use up the oxygen as they work to break down all the dead plants. Without oxygen, fish and other pond animals die.

Many people are working to protect ponds. Scientists are studying how pollution affects the plants and animals. They are finding ways to clean up the water and keep the algae under control. Volunteer groups are helping, too. They are cleaning out ponds that are choked with weeds or garbage. They are building new ponds in gardens and schoolyards. If we all treat ponds with care, these small, busy worlds will always be there for us to explore and enjoy.

# FAST FACTS ABOUT PONDS

**LOCATION:** Everywhere in the world, except at the North Pole or South Pole.

**SIZE:** Ponds are generally smaller and shallower than lakes, but there is no accepted definition of the different sizes of lakes and ponds.

**TEMPERATURES:** Water temperatures vary depending on the place, season, and time of day. The lowest temperatures are usually just before sunrise and the highest temperatures at sunset.

**PLANTS FOUND IN NEW YORK PONDS:** *Swamp zone:* Tall, upright plants, including grasses, reeds, rushes, horsetails, and cattails. *Floating leaf zone:* Rooted plants with leaves floating on the surface or just beneath it, including water lilies and water plantains. *Submerged plant zone:* Rooted plants that grow almost completely underwater, including waterweeds, water milfoils, and water violets. *Free-floating plant zone:* Free-floating plants, including duckweeds, bladderworts, and frogbits. Plantlike *algae* and *fungi* live throughout the pond.

**ANIMALS FOUND IN NEW YORK PONDS:** *Insects* include backswimmers, butterflies, craneflies, damselflies, dragonflies, horseflies, midges, mosquitoes, springtails, water boatmen, water measurers, water scorpions, water striders, and whirligig beetles. *Fish* include carp, catfish, perch, pickerel, pike, sticklebacks, sunfish, and trout. *Mollusks* include freshwater mussels and pond snails. *Crustaceans* include copepods, freshwater shrimp (also called side-swimmers), seed shrimp, and water fleas. *Reptiles* include northern water snakes, painted turtles, and snapping turtles. *Birds* include belted kingfishers, Canada geese, golden-winged warblers, great blue herons, Mallard ducks, mute swans, and red-shouldered hawks. *Amphibians* include American bullfrogs, northern green frogs, eastern American toads, and spotted salamanders. *Mammals* that visit the pond include American beavers, little brown bats, masked shrews, meadow jumping mice, muskrats, North American raccoons, and white-tailed deer. There are also many *hydras, mites, moss animals, protozoa, rotifers, spiders, sponges,* and *worms.*

# GLOSSARY

**adaptation**—Ways in which living things adapt, or change to survive under the conditions in a certain environment.

**algae (AL-jee)**—Simple plantlike organisms that live mostly in the water.

**amphibians (am-FIH-bee-unz)**—Cold-blooded vertebrates (animals with a backbone) that begin life in the water and live on land as an adult. *Amphibian* means "both lives."

**bacteria (back-TEER-ee-uh)**—Simple living things made up of just one cell, which are usually too small to see without a microscope.

**camouflage (KAM-uh-flaj)**—Coloring or other physical features that help living things blend in with their surroundings, hiding them from other animals.

**carbon dioxide**—A gas that is formed when animals breathe and dead plants and animals decay. Plants use carbon dioxide in photosynthesis.

**community**—All the plants and animals that live in an ecosystem and depend on one another for survival.

**decomposers**—Creatures that feed on dead plant and animal matter and release the nutrients back into the ecosystem.

**ecosystem**—An area that is home to a particular community of plants and animals, which are specially suited to living in that environment. An ecosystem includes all the living things of the area plus all the nonliving things, such as the temperature, water, and rocks.

**floating leaf zone**—The area of the pond where the water is deeper than the swamp zone but shallower than the submerged plant zone. Most of the plants are rooted in the mud, with leaves that float on the surface.

**food chain**—The path of food energy from one living thing to another.

**food web**—A collection of many overlapping food chains.

**free-floating plant zone**—The part of the pond where plants that are not rooted in the mud float at or just beneath the surface. This zone often occurs in the deepest waters, but the plants sometimes spread over large areas of the surface.

**fungi (FUN-guy)**—Small plantlike organisms such as mold, which feed on living and dead plants and animals. The word for one of these organisms is *fungus*.

**gills**—A part of a water creature's body that is used mainly for breathing and sometimes for filtering food from the water.

**mammal**—An animal that is warm-blooded, breathes air, and nurses its young with milk.

**metamorphosis (met-uh-MORE-fuh-sus)**—The series of major changes, from stage to stage, that some animals go through as they develop from babies into adults.

**nocturnal**—Active mainly at night.

**nutrients (NOO-tree-uhnts)**—Substances that are taken in by plants and animals to help them live and grow.

**nymphs (nimfs)**—The young form of many insects, including dragonflies.

**oxygen (AHK-sih-jun)**—An element that is found in the air and water. Almost all living things need oxygen to survive.

**photosynthesis (foe-toe-SIN-thuh-sus)**—The process by which plants use energy from sunlight to combine water and carbon dioxide to make food.

**plankton**—Masses of very small plants and animals that float in bodies of water. The plants are called *phytoplankton* (FIE-toe-plank-ton), and the animals are called *zooplankton* (zoh-uh-PLANK-ton).

**pond**—A small, shallow body of still water.

**predator**—An animal that hunts and kills other animals for food.

**prey**—An animal that is hunted by a predator.

**species (SPEE-sheez)**—Specific types of plants and animals.

**submerged plant zone**—The area between the floating leaf zone and the center of the pond, where the plants are rooted in the bottom and grow almost completely underwater.

**surface tension**—A property of water and other liquids that causes the surface of the liquid to behave like a thin elastic film or skin.

**swamp zone**—The area of the pond that is closest to the shore, where tall, upright plants grow.

**zones**—The areas of a pond. Each zone has its own special conditions and is home to its own types of plants.

# FIND OUT MORE

## Books

Fleisher, Paul. *Lake and Pond Food Webs*. Minneapolis: Lerner Publications, 2008.

Hibbert, Adam. *Life in a Pond*. New York: Gareth Stevens, 2010.

Kallen, Stuart A. *Life in a Pond*. San Diego: KidHaven Press, 2004.

Pascoe, Elaine. *Pond*. San Diego: Blackbirch Press, 2005.

Ridley, Sarah. *Minibeasts in a Pond*. Mankato, MN: Smart Apple Media, 2010.

## Websites

### Biomes-Habitats: Pond Life Animal Printouts

www.enchantedlearning.com/biomes/pond/pondlife.shtml

This Enchanted Learning site has lots of printable pictures and activity sheets for learning about the animals that live in and around ponds.

### Exploring Pond Habitats

www.naturegrid.org.uk/pondexplorer/pond-cross.html

Click on the "mini-habitats" to find out about the animals that live in different parts of the pond.

### Ponds and Lakes

www.mbgnet.net/fresh/lakes/index.htm

Follow the links to learn about lakes and ponds and the plants and animals that live in them. This colorful site is presented by the Missouri Botanical Garden.

### A Virtual Pond Dig

http://microscopy-uk.org.uk/index.html?http://microscopy-uk.org.uk/pond/

Take a dip in a virtual jar to learn about some of the tiny creatures found in pond water.

### World Biomes: Freshwater

http://kids.nceas.ucsb.edu/biomes/freshwater.html

This Kids Do Biology site explores the plants, animals, and people that depend on freshwater ecosystems such as lakes and ponds.

# INDEX

Page numbers in **boldface** are illustrations.

# ABOUT THE AUTHOR

**VIRGINIA SCHOMP** has written more than eighty books for young readers on topics including dinosaurs, dolphins, world history, American history, myths, and legends. She lives among the tall pines of New York's Catskill Mountain region. When she is not writing books, she enjoys hiking, gardening, baking (and eating!) cookies, watching old movies and new anime, and, of course, reading, reading, and reading.

# PHOTO CREDITS

The photographs in this book are used by permission and through the courtesy of:

*Front cover:* Courtesy of Alan Tsai.

*Alamy:* Brian Elliott, 1; Don Johnston, 4; Wildlife, 6; blickwinkel/Jagel, 11 (right); Scenics & Science, 13; Malcolm Schuyl, 22; M. Timothy O'Keefe, 24; Mark Conlin, 27; blickwinkel/Hecker, 29; Danita Delimont, 35 (bottom left); georgesanker.com, 37; Linda Freshwaters Arndt, 38; Dominique Braud/Dembinsky Photo Associates, 40. *Getty Images:* Rodger Jackman, 20; William H. Mullins, 26; Charles Krebs, 30. *Superstock:* Universal Images Group, 8; Gary Neil Corbett, 10; Minden Pictures, 11 (left), 19, 21; NHPA, 16, 41; Photononstop, 18; age fotostock, 32; imagebroker.net, 34, 35 (top right).